Step on a Crack

Step on a Crack

Poems by

Marilyn L. Taylor

Kelsay Books

© 2016 Marilyn L. Taylor. All rights reserved. This material may not be reproduced in any form, published, reprinted, recorded, performed, broadcast, rewritten or redistributed without the explicit permission of Marilyn L. Taylor. All such actions are strictly prohibited by law.

Cover photograph: David Graham

ISBN 13- 978-1-945752-21-6

Kelsay Books
White Violet Press
www.kelsaybooks.com

To my husband, David Scheler,
  who rescued me from a dark place

Acknowledgments

My thanks to the editors of the publications in which the following poems, sometimes in slightly different versions, first appeared:

Connotation Press: "A Commencement Villanelle"
Free Verse: "Contingency"
Poemeleon: "Reverie in Sapphics, With Fries" and "How Aunt Eudora Became a Post-Modern Poet"
Poets On: "One Last Favor"
Poet Lore: "What They Don't Know"
Re/Verse: "Family Dynamic"
The Ledge: "Always Questions"
Transactions of the Wisconsin Academy of Sciences, Arts and Letters: "Tercets from the Train"
Verse Wisconsin: "Piano Overture"
Wisconsin Poetry: "The Boy on the Plane"
JMI: Journal of the Motherhood Initiative for Research and Community Involvement: "At the End"

Contents

Step on a Crack: a Charm	11
Piano Overture	12
The Boy on the Plane	13
Tercets from the Train	14
Dismay	16
What They Don't Know	17
Compulsory Figures	18
Always Questions	19
A Commencement Villanelle	20
Reverie in Sapphics, With Fries	21
How Aunt Eudora Became a Post-Modern Poet	22
Open Letter to Grownup Kids Who Call Home	23
For Max at Five Months	24
Reading Alcott, 1962	25
Miss Dixie's Proud Mama	26
The Belgian Half	27
Lonely as a Cloud	28
Message from the Ice Cave	29
This is the Poem that I Could Never Write	30
Family Dynamic	31
A Sestina for My Mother	32
From a Dark Place	34
Contingency	35
The Good Daughter, 1963	36
One Last Favor	37
At the End	38
Autobiography as Oxymoron	39
If, in October	40
The Foreigner	41

About the Author

Step on a Crack: a Charm

Step on a crack,
bring your mother back
from the dark caves of retrospect,
and your own benign neglect.

Bow to her,
as if she were the girl
of twenty-two
who once gave birth to you.

See her pale eyes
widen in surprise
as if she can't believe
how profoundly you still grieve.

Now pronounce her name
so she can reclaim
what has become of you,
her child, her heir, her feckless residue.

Piano Overture

He came to our apartment twice a year
to tune my mother's piano. All day long
we tiptoed, trying not to interfere
with what to us were strange, unearthly songs.

He never struck a heavy, luscious chord—
only fifths, fourths, octaves—clean and spare;
brandishing his hammer like a sword,
we watched him wring concordance from the air.

Taut as pulled wire, he'd lean into the keys,
his practiced fingers pressing note on note,
hunting down aberrant harmonies
and any latent quaver in the throat.

At last the piano, gaping and undone,
its very heart exposed for all to see,
would wait in silence, chastened as a nun,
for the blasphemies of Chopin and Satie.

The Boy on the Plane

The boy on the plane is coming home
from his grandfather's funeral—his first
exposure to the way it's done, how we comb
and scrub and manicure and dress
the body, wiping away the evidence
of life's final squalor. He stares into his lap,
while a half-dream plays along his lips.

On either side of us, the clouds
are climbing into mounded, coalescing
heaps—how voluptuous they look, viewed from the side,
their secret folds and cumulations riding
on shafts of wild, sliding
air. Yawning enormously, the boy turns and smiles
with pleasure at the girl across the aisle.

I think about old men, and of the boy
beside me, how it's almost time
for him; and of the girl he will someday
press against in a cool, darkened room.
And the heaviness I've known
before, that profound wrenching I recognize
grinds forward, and settles into place.

Tercets from the Train

Human dramas implode without trace.
    —Marge Piercy

Gorgeous, they are gorgeous, these two women getting
    on the train, one in lime green silk, black hair
        a mile wide, the other slim as a whip, coiled

in red linen. Their two small boys, grinning,
    have squirmed into facing seats, bubbling with spare
        energy, the cuffs of their designer jeanlets rolled

at the ankles, their studded shirts glinting.
    I overhear the women talking over what to wear
        to some convention (should it be the gold

Armani or the St. Laurent?) while the boys are gazing
    through the rain-spattered window, practicing their
        locomotive lingo in shrill, five-year-old

voices, demanding information: are we going
    faster than a plane, where is the engineer,
        does this train have electricity or coal?

But the women's eyes are fierce, they are grumbling
    over Lord & Taylor, which was once a store
        to be reckoned with, although the one with wild

hair points out that even Bloomingdale's is growing
    more K-Martish than it ever was before.
        Don't you interrupt me, child,

she hisses to the boy who wonders why the train is grinding
    so slowly through the towns, and where
        the bathroom is and what the ticket-man is called

until she bends over him, glaring
    from beneath her shadowed eyes, a crimson flare
        on either cheek. *You're interrupting me*, she growls.

Now you'll be sorry. His mouth is gaping
    as the flat of her hand splits the air,
        annihilating two long rows of smiles.

I warned you, didn't I, darling?
    Now don't you dare cry. Don't you dare.
        Up and down the aisle, the silence howls.

Dismay

He had been watching the world open up to him under the sun, ever since as a baby the light refined itself to mother and father and moon and toy and grass in the front yard. His eyes were little wildflowers that flew and seeded themselves, alighting and germinating in unlikely spots. Soon he was taken to plays for children and later to concerts, where another child, a little older, was holding beneath her chin a tiny violin and producing from it a sound that enchanted him, in part because that small child, that miniature, had created it and he wanted to do that too, to make a sound like hers on the violin. When the instrument was provided and he went off to the place that showed children how to make those sweet sounds, all he could muster was a screech, a squawk, a gravelly scratch that bore no resemblance to what he'd heard. He kept at it for weeks, but there was still only gravel, only scratches, no silk; only burlap and raspy woolen noise. And it was then that he saw the first cloud, the first covering of a small part of the sun, and understood what he could not be.

What They Don't Know

They are thirteen, all flying elbows
and thinbone knees, wrapping their tongues
around words like *pimp* and *bare-ass*
and *hard-on.* They are astounded
by girls, the bodies of girls, the onrush
of lips and hair, and they talk about
what it would be to touch one of those
flashy breasts, to look it in the eye.

They are thirteen, and they don't know
about the Buick they might be riding in
a year or two from now, packed in hip-to-hip
chanting a frenzied *go go go go*
until the pavement starts to bulge
and crest, lifting them, sending them up
into some kind of heartstop heaven.

They don't know that the tree might be an elm
that the car will wrap itself around
in lascivious embrace, or that afterwards
a thin, watery sigh *Open the door*
could be the first sound and the last
before sirens take up the threnody.

For now, though, they lean lightly
on their slender bikes, polishing
a new language: *horny, piss-off, kiss my ass.*
Expertly they palm their cigarettes,
the thick smoke streaming
from their mouths and noses.

Compulsory Figures

I know you don't remember this at all,
but Daddy used to love to take us skating,
and you would always have a fit—creating
havoc so he'd drive us home. You'd bawl
your head off just as he was teaching me
some elegant new leap, a camel-spin,
and then your little passion-play kicked in.
But I was twelve and gawky, you were three
and cute, so I was powerless. Suffice
to say that people might have looked askance
if I had grabbed you by the ruffled pants
and Tonya Harding'ed you across the ice.
But now that you're a dainty forty-two,
I wouldn't *dream* of doing that to you.

Always Questions

*Yesterday at the mall? I bought a book
of Emily Dickinson? For my mom?*
              —overheard at Starbucks

There is a moment, in the middle teens,
when virtually every sentence ends
on an upward curl, as if it really means
to be a question—or at least pretends

to entertain an element of doubt—
like this: *I started early? Took my dog?*
implying that I may have ventured out
exceptionally *late*, to take a jog

without the dog, or anyone else, along.
And if I add: *and visited the sea?*—
I'm hinting that of course I could be wrong
about this "sea" thing, ha-ha, you know me.

It's evidently hard for them to say
the thing they mean, without a little cue
for feedback, for the understood *Okay*;
or, possibly, they talk the way they do

because they are the representatives
of a long-out-of-date civility—
these gentle souls who speak in tentatives,
and always dwell in possibility.

A Commencement Villanelle

I'd like to tell him something he should know
on this momentous day—his graduation.
I don't think he's going to like it, though.

He'll claim he heard that sermon long ago,
why can't I rid myself of my fixation,
quit mouthing things I think he ought to know?

He's certain that I'll tell him *Take it slow.*
Do all your messing up in moderation.
He's right. And he won't like it much. Although

he'll like it better than the way I'll go
mano a mano, some smooth variation
on all the things he doesn't know I know—

like where he hides his stash from Mexico
and other shortcuts to intoxication
beneath the basement stairs. He'll deny it, though.

Still, I'll avoid that burning down below,
exclude all references to fornication,
even small precautions. (Like he doesn't know?)

And that's my make-believe scenario,
my grand conclusion to his education:
I'll tell him everything he needs to know.
He'll barely listen. That won't stop me, though.

Reverie in Sapphics, with Fries

Straight-spined girl—yes, you of the glinting earrings,
amber skin and sinuous hair: what happened?
you've no business lunching with sticky children
here at McDonald's.

Are they yours? How old were you when you had them?
You are far too dazzling to be their mother,
though I hear them spluttering *Mommy Mommy*
over the Muzak.

Do you plan to squander your precious twenties
wiping ice cream dripping from little fingers,
drowning your ennui in a Dr. Pepper
from the dispenser?

Were I you for one schizophrenic moment,
I'd display my pulchritude with a graceful
yet dismissive wave to the gathered burghers
feeding their faces—

find myself a job as a super-model,
get me to those Peloponnesian beaches
where I'd preen all day with a jug of ouzo
in my bikini.

Would I miss the gummy suburban vinyl,
hanker for the Happiest Meal on Main Street?
Or would one spectacular shrug suffice for
begging the question?

How Aunt Eudora Became a Post-Modern Poet

A girl is not supposed to write that way
(the teachers told her in the seventh grade)—
you ought to find more proper things to say.

For instance, there's no reason to portray
your daddy sucking gin like lemonade—
young girls are not supposed to write that way.

And we don't care to read an exposé
on how your mama gets the grocer paid;
there ought to be more proper things to say.

Why not write about a nice bouquet
of flowers, or a waterfall, instead?
You cannot be allowed to write the way

you did, for instance, when your Uncle Ray
was entertaining strangers in his bed,
and what the county sheriff had to say.

Why put such vulgar passions on display?
You're going to regret it, I'm afraid—
remember, you're a girl. So *write* that way.
Go find yourself some proper things to say.

Open Letter to Grownup Kids Who Call Home

It's not that we don't like it when you phone us—
it's wonderful to have you on the line;
we're pleased about your friends, your house, your bonus,
and know we shouldn't worry, you're just fine.

But frankly, we're not worried in the slightest;
we know that you are competent and wise,
and have a place among the best and brightest
survivors of spaghettios and fries.

But lately we have other obligations,
the stuff that we have time (at last) to do—
it could be work, it could be recreation,
but hasn't got a thing to do with you.

It might involve a cruise to Casablanca
or biking from Saint Cloud to Saskatoon
or teaching social science in Sri Lanka
or going bowling every afternoon

So when you call to say you've done it Your Way,
you're doing great, we're listening to you—
but even so, our eyes are on the doorway
that in a minute we'll be bolting through.

For Max at Five Months

Hey, little handful,
beamish baby, super-napper,
better hold onto that smile—
there's a toddler hiding right beside you,
and only a moon or two away, a boy
with a book and a bike.

Can you guess
where they're headed?
Just around the corner, where
a young man stretched out on the grass
is contemplating a blue sky
filled with sailing ships.

As soon as you have learned
how to stand on your own
two feet you'll set off after them,
and one by one they will take
you in. You will grow more
and more invisible.

You won't even remember
being here, grinning at us
in pure, oblivious bliss—
where nothing interrupts
the present, or foreshadows
the great events to come.

Reading Alcott, 1962

Of course I knew she wrote the whole thing
about a hundred years ago, when people were
a lot more used to that kind of dismal stuff.
But by chapter 36 it was pretty clear to me
that Beth was going to die (and really soon).
I couldn't stand it. *"Louisa May!"* I cried out
from the depths of my soul, *"How could you
do this? How could you kill her?"*

And then I'd think about my own sister Pam
with her orange bangs and denim pedal-pushers
stretched out in a four-poster bed under a faded quilt.
She'd be way too weak for needlework by now,
so I'd bring her chamomile tea in a china cup
and bend over her counterpane in my long, dark
dress (what's a counterpane, anyway?) crooning
something like, *"The New Years Eve we did the town,
the day we tore the goalposts down,"* and Pam
would shoot me a trembly smile and slurp some tea.

"Read me a story," she would beg, "to guide me
to the promised land." So I'd take my grimy copy
of *Tropic of Cancer* out of my pocket and read to her
from the best parts. She'd ask me to read some of them
again and again. Then she'd close her eyes
and we would speak quietly of the cute new boy
who'd moved into the house next door. His name
would be Laurie. And then she'd make me promise
that the minute she died I had to go over there
and ask him if he wanted to go to the funeral with me
and take in a movie afterwards. Or a play, or
whatever they had in those days. And I would nod
bravely and say yes, of course I would. Of course.

Miss Dixie's Proud Mama

I've slapped myself three times across the face,
and this time it's not a dream, I swear—
my babygirl has really won First Place
in the beauty contest at State Fair.
Look at how she slinks in those high heels,
cranks her little hips just like a pro
down that runway—honey, she's on wheels,
she's headed for the Johnny Carson show.
Come on, sweetheart, talk a little louder,
bat those lashes, lick your lips a lot;
make your poor old mama even prouder—
grab for what your mama never got.
    Thank you, Jesus; thank you, Maidenform!
    Now watch my baby take the world by storm.

The Belgian Half

Listen, I don't have a grandmother
on that side, never did. Never knew
any bantamweight woman in black kid shoes
stirring blancmange in a darkening kitchen,
ceiling adrip with anise-scented steam.

Couldn't tell you if she cried when her only son
bolted for New York, sleek little man
with narrow feet, ascot, nostrils on the move—
don't know if she heard about his plans to marry,
which he did (skinny lady in an ermine coat)

Or that he'd fathered a child,
so I've no idea if there might have been
grief in that kitchen or a wrinkled hand to hold,
to comfort in its coldest hour, with *Viens, viens,
Mémé—I am the daughter of your boy.*

Lonely as a Cloud

So here they are,
exactly one month to the day
after your funeral—
those goddamn daffodils
you planted last fall.

Message from the Ice Cave

for Rachel, after the death of her young daughter

I am living here now, where the cold
is my consort, the lover I clasp
with my arms and legs, from whose gray
blanket I tear each breath.

All around me ice is in bloom—
tiny glass buds keep swelling
from hairline fissures
in the stone. The buried river

cuts close, a dark ventricle
thick with sorrow. Moisture floods
my face, pools at my feet.
In time, a tower of ice

will grow around me, taking
the shape of an old woman
and visitors will say, *Look at her,
how she weeps into her hands.*

This is the Poem that I Could Never Write

This is the poem
about a dog
that I never could write

This is the poem
I never could write
about a dog
chasing a squirrel

This is the poem
about the dog
who chased a squirrel
right into the street
who hit the
that I never could write

This is also a poem
about the truck

This is the poem
that I never could write
about a dog who

This is the poem
about the dog
who chased a squirrel
into the street
who hit the

It is also a poem
about a truck.

Family Dynamic

Mel, Mel, the dad from hell
Raised your kids in a padded cell;
Not one soul cried the night you died,
But Mother giggled like a bride.

A Sestina for My Mother

We never mentioned dying, she and I;
never spoke of passing on, growing old
with grace, wearing lipstick to the last
emergency, all that. But she died. Because
of cigarettes, they said, but I knew better—
her inner fire, untended, guttered out.

When she lay sick, the news had not come out
about the changes (neither she nor I
had seen them coming.) Not knowing any better,
we worried that she'd broken all the old
rules, flouted ancient customs, because
she hadn't done her penance first, her dying last.

But he's Attila, she hissed to me at last;
*he's Norman Bates, before they dragged him out
of the cellar. Benedict Arnold, because
he turned on me. He was Pinkerton, I
the idiot Butterfly. I'll stab the old
bastard through the heart when I get better.*

But she never did get better,
she got weaker, and her fury didn't last;
her face took on the thick sheen of old
ivory as she let herself run out
of time. She could not know that I
was dying too—the nice I, the I she knew—because

I seemed, next to her, so alive. Because
I was getting stronger, better,
even as she blurred and faded. Even as I
saw her breaking up, receding with the last

yellow shreds of sun. Snuffed out.
But me, me—I'm rekindled by old

fires. I burn. I have become the wicked old
witch. I am Grendel's mother, because
of her pain. I am the bat out
of Hell. I am Goneril, or better
still, Hecate. And with my wild torch, I
will light her way at last.

(And you'd better not howl, old
man, or beg with your last shout—because
I'm coming, here I come, to cut your black heart out.)

From a Dark Place

Who are you, child, still floating
in my daughter's womb? I didn't know you
in my time, yet you look like me—
there is a flare to the nostril and a crimp
to the hair that is ours.

Your eyes are sealed like mine,
but your mouth opens and closes
with incipient messages—
if I should whisper back
you would listen, spinning with delight.

Unfold your fingers, if you can—
they are waiting to grow eloquent
and strong. They will move under mine
the first time you touch the watered silk
of an iris, or your mother's face.

Your bed narrows, your bones
are bonding as mine fall
to powder. Soon we will glide away
from one another—you won't remember
passing me in the dissolving dark.

But you have my gifts:
the chromata of our past, strung jewels
I harbored for you all my life.
Without their weight, I vanish
just as you, moon-drenched, appear.

Contingency

> *The minimum lethal dose of morphine is 200 milligrams, typically fourteen light blue 15 mg tablets. Unconsciousness usually occurs in 5 to 15 minutes, death in 20 to 50.* —*www.fineorsuperfine.com*

As soon as the sun departs the house
At five in the afternoon
He deposits and seals in an amber jar
Another pale-blue moon.

He places the jar on the cabinet shelf
And swivels the handle tight;
Pockets the key in his terrycloth robe
And sits and waits for night.

He can hear the grandchildren crowing below,
Awash in their video games;
He tries for a time to assemble their faces,
And say a few of their names.

But he can't recall how many he has,
Or what their small fantasies are,
Or why their mothers and fathers have come
To put his clothes in the car.

He careens on the edge of a desperate thought,
A glimmer from where he's been—
But he doesn't remember the amber jar
Nor the moons crumbling within.

The Good Daughter, 1963

Nobody will ever want me more
than my sullen, shrinking parents do;
they think the very fact that I was born
proves I owe them both a thing or two.
So I've become the daughter that they crave—
the loyal and obedient retainer
who brings them what they need to stay alive
and well—from laxatives to Sunday dinner.
I listen to them re-arrange the past
to suit themselves (their favorite diversion)
and see to it they fall asleep at last,
allowing me an evening for submersion
in that alarming book I bought last week:
something called *The Feminine Mystique*.

One Last Favor

Why yes,
there is something
you can do for us
before you die.
You can please quit
grieving. Stop

leaking out all over us
your sorrow and your
dread. It's hard
for us to watch,
we don't like it,

we would so much rather
have you smiling like
a picture of Saint Jude,
stroking our hands and
telling us *There there,*

this was to be expected.
But with your whole spine
gone bent like that and
your head shaking back
and forth, your eyelids

stiff with fear and every
wasted muscle straining
to deny, deny—just where
are we supposed to turn
for comfort now?

At the End

In another time, a linen winding sheet
would already have been drawn
about her, the funeral drums by now

would have throbbed their dull tattoo
into the shadows writhing
behind the fire's eye

while a likeness
of her narrow torso, carved
and studded with obsidian

might have been passed from hand
to hand and rubbed against the bellies
of women with child

and a twist of her gray hair
been dipped in oil
and set alight, releasing the essence

of her life's elixir, pricking
the nostrils of her children
and her children's children

whose amber faces nod and shine
like a ring of lanterns
strung around her final flare—

but instead, she lives in this white room
gnawing on a plastic bracelet
as she is emptied, filled and emptied.

Autobiography as Oxymoron

Hard as we try
to stick to the truth,
our life stories
are mostly fiction.

To call them the truth
without embellishment
is either fiction
or wishful thinking—

and any embellishment
will conjure stories
of wishful thinking
artfully re-arranged—

stories conjured
straight out of bedlam,
to arrange again
into tidy plots.

Is bedlam still bedlam
when told as a tale?
Will our tidy plots
twist the events,

merely tell tales?
And who will mind
if we twist the events,
avoid the truth?

Who will know
that our own life stories
do not tell the truth,
hard as we try?

If, in October

I should be driving past a row
of brick-and-shingle bungalows
when maple leaves are sticking to the sidewalk,
and a rain-glossed school bus starts to swing
its yellow bulk around the corner,

there you are again—framed in a wavy
leaded window, watering a long-fingered
philodendron while the Victrola
clatters out Landowska's version of
the *Little Preludes* through the glass

and I am nine years old—and you,
the center of my small universe,
are the love of my life, to whose powdered
presence I come home blissfully,
day after dangerous day

utterly innocent of a distant time
when you will turn from me
and withdraw into my archive of losses.
Even your quaint name, *Alice,* melts
to nearly nothing on my tongue.

The Foreigner

I've abandoned my century
and entered another that is not mine.
I'm a stranger here

among hordes of graceful natives
all smooth of skin and lean of memory,
who just a day or two ago

were pounding in the sandbox with
the backs of their shovels.
In the time it's taken

to put away their diapers
they have named a new galaxy
after themselves

choreographed a tango
for silicon chip and atom,
added postmodern cantos

to civilization's epic—
while I have learned
to pick and fumble

through crumbling landmarks,
asking the way to the ruins
in the wrong language.

About the Author

Marilyn L. Taylor, Ph.D., is the former Poet Laureate of the state of Wisconsin and the city of Milwaukee, and the author of six poetry collections. Her poems and essays have appeared in many anthologies and journals, including *Poetry, Light, Measure, Able Muse*, and the Random House anthology titled *Villanelles*. She has been awarded First Place in a number of national and international poetry contests, most recently the international Margaret Reid Award for verse in forms.

Taylor currently lives in Madison, Wisconsin, and regularly facilitates independent poetry workshops and presentations nearby, statewide, and elsewhere—including programs sponsored by Lawrence University, Western State Colorado University, Poetry by the Sea in Connecticut, and the University of Wisconsin-Madison's Division of Continuing Studies.

Made in the USA
Middletown, DE
01 October 2016